It's Easy To B
Metal Guitar

by Joe Bennett

Exclusive Distributors:
Music Sales Limited
8/9 Frith Street, London W1V 5TZ, England.
Music Sales Corporation
257 Park Avenue South, New York, NY10010, USA.
Music Sales Pty Limited
120 Rothschild Avenue, Rosebery, NSW 2018, Australia.

Order No. AM955207
ISBN 0-7119-8007-1
This book © Copyright 2000 Wise Publications

Written by Joe Bennett.
Edited by Sorcha Armstrong.
Musical examples by Richard Barrett.
Music processed by Digital Music Art.

Book design by Phil Gambrill.
Cover design by Michael Bell Design.
Illustrations by Andy Hammond.

Specialist guitar pictures supplied courtesy of
Balafon Books (pages 93, 96)
Text photographs courtesy of London Features International.

Printed in the United Kingdom by
Printwise (Haverhill) Limited, Haverhill, Suffolk.

Your Guarantee of Quality:
As publishers, we strive to produce
every book to the highest commercial standards.
The music has been freshly engraved and the book has
been carefully designed to minimise awkward page turns
and to make playing from it a real pleasure.
Particular care has been given to specifying acid-free,
neutral-sized paper made from pulps which have not
been elemental chlorine bleached.
This pulp is from farmed sustainable forests and
was produced with special regard for the environment.
Throughout, the printing and binding have been
planned to ensure a sturdy, attractive publication
which should give years of enjoyment.
If your copy fails to meet our high standards, please
inform us and we will gladly replace it.

Music Sales' complete catalogue describes thousands
of titles and is available in full colour sections by subject,
direct from Music Sales Limited.
Please state your areas of interest and send
a cheque/postal order for £1.50 for postage to: Music Sales Limited,
Newmarket Road, Bury St. Edmunds, Suffolk IP33 3YB.

www.musicsales.com

It's Easy To Bluff...
Metal Guitar

by Joe Bennett

Wise Publications
London / New York / Paris / Sydney / Copenhagen / Madrid / Tokyo

Introduction 7
The History of Metal 8
Types of Metal 9
The Bands...

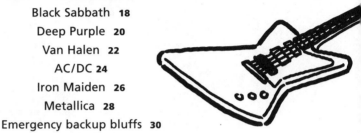

Music and TAB Guide 34
The Music...

Music Shop Classic 89
Guitar Sounds...

Outro 96

Black Sabbath – The Godfathers of Metal

Introduction

Anyone who's ever picked up an electric guitar has tried to 'play heavy' at one time or another. However seriously you study, however much you learn your scales and modes, there's nothing like the feeling you get standing in front of an eight-speaker stack with a ringing 'A' power chord vibrating through your boots. Guitarists discovered this sometime in the mid-'60s, and ever since then, metal acts have been vying with each other to become the heaviest, the dirtiest, the LOUDEST band on the block.

Only trouble is - playing the guitar is *difficult*, and some say it even takes *practice*! Fear not, O disciple of all things metallic. *It's Easy To Bluff... Metal Guitar* is here.

This book will show you all the riffs, licks and tricks you need to become a true metal master. But more importantly, it also gives you the absolute essentials of heavy guitar playing – the gear to buy, the albums to listen to, and the guitarists to mention. In no time at all you'll become an expert in evil, a graduate of grind and a monarch of mosh.

For example

Guitarists naturally have a tendency to judge each other by technical skill. The metal bluffer need show no fear, even when confronted with the most well-practised virtuoso. Any rival who can play stunning sweep-picking arpeggios at 10 notes per second can be dismissed as 'passé', 'retro', or 'a heavy metal dinosaur'. Players who achieve super-accurate scalic runs should be accused of 'having no feel' or 'missing the point'.

Of course, if you get stuck in a situation when your playing really is on the line, we've helpfully supplied just a smattering of impressive musical examples which you can throw into solos whenever you think the audience need reminding of your complete mastery of the instrument.

Worshippers will build effigies of you and sacrifice small mammals to your name. And grandparents will warn their children to behave, in case they turn out like you. Or at the very least, you'll impress them down the King's Arms on Friday night. The choice is yours, true believer...

The History Of Metal or 'How To Start A Fight In A Rock Bar'

If you're going to get maximum credibility among the metal fraternity, you've got to know your history. Contemporary bands like Slayer, Primus and Fear Factory acknowledge their debt to the ancients by appearing on stage with Ozzy Osborne. And any guitarist who doesn't own the debut album 'Van Halen' is almost certainly a wuss-ass wimp-out jazz player (in which case, you're reading the wrong book – get *It's Easy To Bluff... Jazz Guitar* instead).

The first band to use the words 'Heavy Metal' were '60s veterans **Steppenwolf** in the rock classic 'Born To Be Wild' (it's the second line of verse 2, trivia fans), but the term wasn't in proper use until 1970, when **Black Sabbath** released their classic debut album *Paranoid*.

Since then, the style has enjoyed hundreds of different interpretations and re-definitions. It forgot to do any guitar practice and called itself Punk. It took a holiday in the USA and became Soft Rock. It got played at 45rpm got re-titled Thrash. Some Christians changed the lyrics and it became White. Even when we all ran out of names for it in the early '90s, someone came up with Alternative Metal.

The following pages contain everything you need to know about the various types of music that go around calling themselves 'Metal'. The text has been especially designed to be as controversial as possible, thus starting fights in rock bars and generally cementing your reputation as a Hard Man (or Woman) of Metal. And if someone challenges you on any of these opinions, stick to your guns... unless you think you're likely to come off worse in a fight. Hey, I never said this book was foolproof...

Ozzy Osbourne

Types Of Metal

Blues-rock

Jimmy Page

BORN: 1965-66

DIED: Never!

SOUND: Psychedelic 'power trio' lineup, busy & chaotic drum parts, bass & guitar riffs in unison.

LYRICS: Drug references and random visual imagery mixed with classic blues sentiments, e.g. "Gotta take one more pill babeeeee... 'cos the sky's gone turquoise... and they repossessed my goddam car..."

BANDS: Jimi Hendrix Experience, Cream, Led Zeppelin, AC/DC, early **Whitesnake**

NOTES: Never confuse Blues-rock with Classic Metal, however much they might sound the same.

Led Zeppelin spent most of their career denying they were a heavy metal band, and **Clapton** soon turned down the volume controls on his Marshalls.

COOL RATING: 10

Whitesnake

AC/DC

Classic Metal

BORN: 1970

DIED: 1980 - its lifeforce was passed to the NWOBHM (see page 12)

SOUND: Usually two guitars, and sometimes organ. Very riff-driven but more often in a minor key. Every vocalist was influenced by **Led Zeppelin**, except Sabbath's **Ozzy Osborne**, who was influenced by the sound of an air-raid siren.

LYRICS: Evil & satanic imagery, war, death, necromancy etc. Stuff your granny wouldn't like. Unless She Too Had Been Consumed By The Forces Of Darkness...

BANDS: Black Sabbath, Deep Purple, Blue Öyster Cult

NOTES: Of all the classic metal bands, only the mighty **Black Sabbath** can still command cool points.

COOL RATING: 9 (**Black Sabbath**)...
6 (everyone else)

Deep Purple

Prog Rock

BORN: 1972ish

DIED: 1977 (had a fist fight with Punk – who head-butted it out of town)

SOUND: Weird time signatures, key changes, 20-minute epic tracks, flash musicianship played by English public schoolboys.

LYRICS: Still plenty of magic and middle-earth stuff, but much 'nicer' than all that Satanic nastiness. In Prog, the Servants Of Satan become pixies, Necromancers Of Hell become sorcerers, Demons Of The Undead become Santa's elves etc. And they all lived in a pink castle where the dragons could never hurt them.

BANDS: Genesis, Yes, Jethro Tull, Rush, Marillion, Queensrÿche

NOTES: Despite the fact that some of the music is actually quite good, you must never admit even to knowing that Prog exists.
Fans of **Rush, Marillion** and **Queensrÿche** never accepted its death at all.

COOL RATING: 1

Marillion

American Metal

BORN: 1978

DIED: 1985 (when it metamorphosed into Big Girls' Blouse Metal)

SOUND: Chugging eight-to-the-bar palm-muted guitars with loads of delay, squealy vocals, big drum sounds. Occasional keyboards.

LYRICS: As bland as possible. Even "My baby likes to love me all night long" is a bit too specific. Try "My baby likes to rock... quite a lot...". If anyone starts to understand the words it's probably time for a guitar solo.

BANDS: Van Halen, Motley Crüe, Bon Jovi, Aerosmith

NOTES: Hugely influential because it made metal chart-friendly. But what price was paid?

COOL RATING:
8 (**Van Halen** and **Aerosmith**)...
4 (everyone else)

Aerosmith & Bon Jovi

Punk

BORN: 1976

DIED: 1980, when it collided with pop and became New Wave. Thrash had a baby with Punk and they named it Hardcore, but that's another story...

RESURRECTED: 1993, when various Seattle bands played some quiet bits on the verses and re-named it Grunge.

SOUND: Big strummed barre chords through plenty of amp distortion. Played with plenty of attitude and an inversely proportional amount of accuracy.

LYRICS: Although Punk was originally based on political angry whinging ('the government are all Fascists but The Kids are cool'), it spent some time with bland Americans in the '80s and turned into more straightforward angry whinging ('The Kids are cool and the government... doesn't understand The Kids').

BANDS: Sex Pistols, The Clash, The Damned, The Ramones ('70s), **Nirvana, Soundgarden, Green Day, Offspring** ('90s)

NOTES: Punk may not currently be a fashionable term, but without it there probably wouldn't be any heavy music in the current charts at all.

COOL RATING: 3 ('70s bands)... 9 (everyone else)

NWOBHM (New Wave Of British Heavy Metal)

BORN: 1980

DIED: 1983

SOUND: Bluesy riffs with screeching vocals. Lots of guitars!

LYRICS: Varied. **Maiden** continued with the death/necromancy theme. **Saxon** made macho references to fights, cars, and girls. **Def Leppard** borrowed from emerging trends in American metal and helped to develop Big Girls' Blouse Metal.

BANDS: Judas Priest, Iron Maiden, Saxon, Samson, Def Leppard

NOTES: Denim and leather collided in what was, after punk, the most unwashed incarnation of metal.

COOL RATING: 3

Iron Maiden

Big Girls' Blouse Metal aka:
Soft Rock, 'AOR' (Adult Oriented Rock), Pop-rock

BORN: 1985

DIED: 1993

SOUND: There are guitars in there, but they're buried by fizzy keyboard parts, nine-part vocal harmonies, and the 'swish' of the singer's curly perm.

LYRICS: As bland as American Metal, but more mentions of Love and Relationships.

BANDS: Late '80s **Bon Jovi** and **Whitesnake, Foreigner, Michael Bolton, Europe, Def Leppard, Bryan Adams**

NOTES: Much derided by Metal devotees, but responsible for some of the biggest-selling Rock albums of all time.

COOL RATING: 2

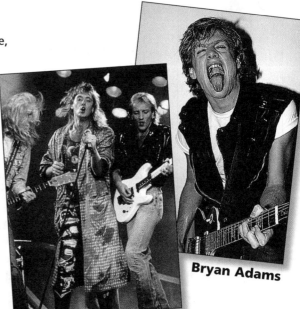

Bryan Adams

Def Leppard

Speed Metal aka: Power Metal, Thrash (many Thrash fans may deny this, of course)

BORN: Motörhead fans say 1976, others agree on about 1985.

DIED: Not yet...

SOUND: Fast. Very fast indeed. Thrash tempos are set purely by how fast the rhythm guitarist can play downstrokes. If the guitarist practises a lot, they become a Speed Metal band.

LYRICS: Difficult to tell at this speed, but let's just say that someone's very angry about something. Swearing in a Thrash lyric is not only big AND clever, it's essential.

BANDS: Megadeth, Anthrax, Venom, Ministry, Slayer, (arguably) **Motörhead, Suicidal Tendencies, Testament, Pantera**

COOL RATING: 7

Megadeth

Instrumental Metal aka: Muso Metal

BORN: 1984, although it was the offspring of several earlier **Frank Zappa** album tracks.

DIED: Mid-1990s, when the album 'Joe Satriani' came out. **Yngwie Malmsteen** refuses to stop recording music, though.

SOUND: Incredibly flash guitar playing.The guitar plays the melody, then takes a... guitar solo. Followed by the melody again. Guitar solo. Middle section melody. Solo. Last section guitar melody. Outro solo.

LYRICS: It's instrumental metal. Why are you reading this bit?

ARTISTS: Joe Satriani, Yngwie Malmsteen, Steve Vai, Steve Morse, Ritchie Kotzen

COOL RATING: 4

Yngwie Malmsteen

Steve Vai

Death Metal, Doom Metal, Black Metal, White Metal, Grindcore aka: Each other...

These terms are great for starting an argument, because fans never agree about what they mean.

Black or Death (i.e. Satanic) Metal was started by **Ozzy** and **Black Sabbath**, and was continued more recently by bands like **Venom**, **Arcturus** and **Emperor** – it's virtually indistinguishable from Doom metal (**Candlemass**, **Witchfinder General**), although Doom tempos tend to be slower. White metal (**Stryper**, **Trouble**) was basically Big Girls' Blouse Metal played by Christians.

Black Sabbath

BORN: At the Dawn Of Metal

DIED: These arguments will never die.

BANDS: Late period **Black Sabbath** (Doom/Black), **Witchfinder General**, **Cathedral** & **Paradise Lost** (Doom/Thrash/Punk), **Mordred**, **King Diamond** & **Venom** (Speed/Thrash) **Sorrow** & **Crematory** (Death/Doom)

COOL RATING: 6 (or 10 if you can navigate a conversation about how to define **Black Sabbath**)

Cathedral

Venom

Industrial
aka: Rap-Metal, rap-core

BORN: Around 1984

SOUND: Guitars with drum machines and occasional rappers.

LYRICS: As any other style of metal, but without the melody.

BANDS: Killing Joke, Anthrax, Deftones, Korn, Fear Factory, Nine Inch Nails

COOL RATING: 10

Korn

Nine Inch Nails

Alternative Metal

Red Hot Chili Peppers

BORN: Early 1990s

SOUND: Play traditional Metal riffs with Grunge production, add some funk grooves, perhaps some rap, and the odd jazz chord, and you've got a recipe for 'Alternative' metal.

LYRICS: Anything you like as long as it avoids traditional Metal subjects (Satan, Smash-the-State politics, bland love songs. And goblins, of course).

BANDS: Living Colour, Jane's Addiction, Sonic Youth, Faith No More, Red Hot Chili Peppers, Primus, Marilyn Manson

COOL RATING: 11

Washburn-toting **Dimebag Darrell** (Pantera) – he comes up with difficult riff by keeping a guitar in every room of the house. Yes, even the bathroom.

The Bands

Bite-size biogs

Metal is different from rock and blues in one important respect – metal guitarists don't need to become obsessed with string gauges, vintage amp tone and plectrum thickness. What's important is *the band*.

The next few pages give you essential background on six classic Metal bands, including a brief history, some info on the guitarist/s, essential albums to own, plus of course an 'instant opinion' on each one. Combine this with your newfound knowledge of the various styles, and you'll have everything you need to beat those *Kerrang!* readers at their own game.

The HM Band... uncovered

- **THE SINGER:** There are two basic types, 'High' and 'Low'. Originally, 'High' metal singers were the only type – think **Ozzy, Robert Plant, Ian Gillan, Dave Lee Roth** etc. The 1990s and early 21st century has brought us the 'Low' type – Nine Inch Nails' **Trent Reznor**, Pantera's **Philip Anselmo**, Metallica's **James Hetfield**. Generally, the more 'Alternative' the metal, the lower the singer.

- **THE GUITARIST:** Again, recent years have moved us more into deeper territory. Time was, the higher up the neck you could play, the higher your status as a player. People even started buying 36-fret guitars in the 1980s. Now, due to the likes of **Pantera, Soulfly** and **Korn**, detuning is the norm in contemporary metal. Anything beyond the 5th fret is for wusses, dude...

- **THE BASSIST:** After an initial bout of early '70s weediness in bass sounds (**Deep Purple, Rush**, some early **Sabbath**), tones were at their deepest and heaviest in the 1980s. These days industrial and alternative types are favouring fuzz/distorted bass, which takes off some of the bottom end. The Chilis' **Flea**, possibly the 90s' most famous metal bassist, was also one of the era's twangiest.

- **THE DRUMMER:** As everyone else has been going deeper and deeper, drum sounds have been getting lighter and less bass-heavy. The double bass drum sound used in Thrash has got thinner and thinner until on some recordings all you can hear is a clicking noise.

Black Sabbath

HISTORY AND BACKGROUND:

Formed in 1969 in the Midlands (home of many a classic metal band, including **Judas Priest**, **Motörhead**, and **Led Zeppelin**). Originally called **Earth**, changed to **Black Sabbath** in 1969. The 'classic' lineup featured Ozzy Osbourne, though he left in 1979, being replaced by Ronnie James Dio, then (briefly) Ian Gillan.

They split in 1983 and got back together again in the late 1990s with Ozzy, headlining at the annual 'Ozzfest' where contemporary bands like **Slayer** and **Fear Factory** come to pay their respects to the masters. The Sabs were once described by the NME as 'representing the best and worst of heavy metal'. The first and most significant band in the history of Metal.

GUITARIST:

Tony Iommi. Responsible for some of Metal's greatest ever riffs. Check out the intro from 'Paranoid', or the unison riffs from 'N.I.B.' or 'Iron Man'. Frequently plays the entire melody of the song in power chords. Has 'bionic' artificial fingertips fitted to his fretting hand. And he's left-handed – how sinister is that?!!

GEAR:

Black Gibson SG with crucifix inlays, into Laney amps. Iommi's original 'primitive' guitar sound is often described as 'British Metal Tone'. It's high-gain, but with loads of midrange and very little delay. On their more recent material he's moved towards a more ordinary LA-style mid-scoop-with-delay sound.

ESSENTIAL ALBUM:

The debut *Paranoid* must be in your collection, but with the Sabs you really need to own one for each of their classic vocalists. It's also worth getting some of Ozzy's solo stuff – 1981's *Diary of a Madman* (featuring the late Randy Rhoads on guitar) is particularly fine.

METAL MAYHEM:

Ozzy famously bit the head off a live bat during a gig, causing a rabies scare. Rock, and indeed, roll!

FINEST MOMENT:

The pouring rain sound effect with the tolling bell in the background at the start of 'Black Sabbath'. You can't get much more metal than that, matey...

FASCINATING FACT:

Rick Wakeman played keyboards on their 1973 album *Sabbath Bloody Sabbath* (but when they played live, all the keyboard parts were played from backstage – they didn't want to look like wusses, now did they?)

INSTANT OPINION:

"It just wasn't the same after Ozzy left."

ACCEPTABLE CRITICISM:

Iommi's 'twin-lead' (i.e. random) guitar solos on the early stuff. Truly awful.

Deep Purple

HISTORY AND BACKGROUND:

Formed in 1968, and first single was a version of Joe South's 'Hush' (later also covered by Kula Shaker). First few albums with original singer Rod Evans flopped, but new singer Ian Gillan's first album with the band (1970's *Deep Purple In Rock*) was an instant classic. Gillan quit in 1973 and was replaced by future Whitesnake vocalist David Coverdale.

Just over a year later, Blackmore also got fed up with the band and went off to form Rainbow with vocalist Ronnie James Dio (who later replaced Ozzy in **Black Sabbath**, and was later himself replaced by Gillan in the same band).

You following all this? No? Look, it's really easy – I can explain the whole thing in one easy-to-remember sentence for you. Evans starts off in Purple, but is replaced by Gillan, who (before he goes off to form the Ian Gillan band which later simply becomes Gillan) records six albums with the band, but leaves and is replaced by Coverdale (who later forms **Whitesnake** which will also include Purple members Jon Lord and Ian Paice), but then Blackmore wants his own band and so forms **Rainbow** with Dio (who later joined **Sabbath**, then left to form Dio, being replaced by Gillan, who was originally with Purple after Evans). Now have you got it?

GUITARIST:
Ritchie Blackmore. A supremely talented player who was the first Metal guitarist to employ exotic scales and modes into solos.

GEAR:
Trademark white Strat with black pickups and 'scalloped' (hollowed-out) frets, which is also favoured by **Yngwie Malmsteen**. Modified Marshalls.

ESSENTIAL ALBUM:
Deep Purple In Rock is the classic, but the ridiculous *Concerto For Group And Orchestra* (1970) is worth owning if only for comedy value.

FASCINATING FACT:
The line-up of the band changed over the years. Original vocalist Rod Evans left in 1969, and was replaced by... oh, forget it.

INSTANT OPINION:
"It just wasn't the same after Evans, Blackmore, Paice, Lord, Gillan, Glover, Dio, Coverdale and Bolin left."

ACCEPTABLE CRITICISM:
Ritchie Blackmore's current taste for pointy hats and mystic capes is just soooo 15th century...

Van Halen

HISTORY AND BACKGROUND:

Formed in 1973 (originally called **Mammoth**) by brothers Eddie and Alex Van Halen with hyperactive vocalist Dave Lee Roth. Became **Van Halen** after recruiting bassist Michael Anthony in 1974.

Debut album *Van Halen* released in 1978 – first hit was a cover of The Kinks' 'You Really Got Me' (the original is thought by some to be the first ever Metal recording). After six albums Roth left for a solo career (notably employing Steve Vai as session man). New vocalist Sammy Hagar took the band further into mainstream pop-metal. Roth briefly got back together with the band in the late 1990s for a few extra tracks which appeared on a compilation. At one time they were the biggest HM band in the world. The late '90s also saw Gary Cherone (ex-**Extreme**) fill the vocal shoes of Dave Lee and Sammy. The band had to publicly apologise for the quality of the resultant album *Van Halen III*.

GUITARIST:

Eddie Van Halen. Famously popularised (some say invented) fingerboard tapping techniques. Possibly the most influential Metal guitarist of all time, along with Blackmore and Hendrix.

GEAR:
Originally 'hybrid' Strat-type guitar with Marshall stack. Now uses Peavey signature model guitar and '5150' amp.

ESSENTIAL ALBUM:
Debut *Van Halen* is unquestionably the most significant, if only because of the seminal instrumental 'Eruption'. The more synthy *1984* does sound very 'Eighties' but it has some more accomplished guitar work.

METAL MAYHEM:
Dave Lee Roth on stage, performing his famous back-flip without ever losing eye contact with the prettiest girls on the front row.

FINEST MOMENT:
Pick an intro - 'Ain't Talkin' 'Bout Love', 'Panama', and 'Jump' (even when he's playing keyboards EVH can still come up with a good riff).

FASCINATING FACT:
The band once did $20,000 worth of damage at a gig because they weren't supplied with one of their tour specifications - M&Ms with the brown ones taken out.

INSTANT OPINION:
"The greatest American Metal band ever."

ACCEPTABLE CRITICISM:
The album *Van Halen III*. The handy alternative to music.

AC/DC

HISTORY AND BACKGROUND:

Formed early '70s, and had some album success, but breakthrough album was 1977's *Let There Be Rock*. The classic *Highway To Hell* was released in '79 and was singer Bon Scott's last album – he died choking in the back of a car. New singer Brian Johnson sounded similar and has stuck with the band to the present day (although at the time of writing there are rumours of a split). The band have built a career on simple chordal riffs, played with laser-accurate timing on two guitars, over a massive drum sound and squealing vocals.

GUITARIST:

Angus Young – one of the few HM guitarists so famous that he is referred to by his first name only. Others include 'Jimi', 'Eddie' and 'Yngwie' (not too surprising, that last one, considering that there aren't very many other famous Metal guitarists called Yngwie). Brother Malcolm handles rhythm guitar duties.

The secret to the AC/DC guitar sound is not to turn up the gain too much. Both guitarists often play full five- or six-string chords, which would get lost with excessive overdrive. You want a bright tone with plenty of mid and just enough overdrive to make it 'bite'.

GEAR:

On stage, Angus wears a schoolboy cap, shorts, school blazer and tie.
Oh, you mean guitars? 1964 Gibson SG-style Les Paul.

ESSENTIAL ALBUM:

Back In Black was Johnson's first as singer. *Highway To Hell* was Bon Scott's last. Both had Mutt Lange (**Def Leppard**, **Bryan Adams** etc) producing. Both have equally generous dollops of Angus's pentatonic mayhem all over them.

METAL MAYHEM:

Live Cannons!

FINEST MOMENT:

The guitar riff from 'Back In Black' – E, D and A with a twiddly bit. Simple yet brilliant.

FASCINATING FACT:

Angus regularly gets so worked up as a result of his manic guitar acrobatics that he has oxygen cylinders backstage so he can nip off for a quick 'fix' to stop him keeling over.

INSTANT OPINION:

"It's actually really difficult to play with that sense of timing – lots of players just don't get it, man..."

ACCEPTABLE CRITICISM:

Perhaps, just possibly, Angus might be getting a bit old for the schoolboy uniform?

Iron Maiden

HISTORY AND BACKGROUND:

Bass player Steve Harris put the band together in 1976, although after two albums original vocalist Paul Dianno was replaced by ex-**Samson** frontman Bruce Dickinson. Loads of albums incl. *Number Of The Beast*, *Powerslave*, *Live After Death* all had the same formula – improbably high HM vocals with twin lead guitar parts and typical Sabbath-like myth-and-magic imagery. After Dickinson left, they briefly recruited **Wolfsbane** vocalist Blaze Bayley. Now back with Dickinson. Spearheaded the NWOBHM, and kept British Metal alive in the album charts during the mid-1980s, when everyone else was busy buying hairspray and programming synthesisers.

GUITARISTS:

Dave Murray and Adrian Smith. Lots of harmonised twin-lead stuff.

GEAR:

Mostly Fender Strats into Marshalls, although Dave Murray customised his guitar by putting DiMarzio humbuckers in it. Later played an ESP.

ESSENTIAL ALBUM:

Number Of The Beast remains one of their best, although subsequent recordings sounded very similar.

METAL MAYHEM:

'Eddie', the band's cadaverous logo character, was originally a murderer (*Killers*), then was a fighter pilot ('Aces High'), was shot down (probably over Egypt, which might explain the *Powerslave* Sphinx cover artwork), rose from the grave (*Live After Death*), and travelled through history (*Somewhere in Time*). Later took up a career as a soothsayer/mystic (*Seventh Son*). All that and a busy touring schedule too!

FINEST MOMENT:

'Phantom of the Opera' twin guitar intro. As well as being a remarkably typical exemplar of the musicological theorems behind the ensemble, it also, er, rocks.

FASCINATING FACT:

According to rock legend, producer Martin Birch had his car fixed at the time of the *Number Of The Beast* tour. The bill came to exactly £666.66...

INSTANT OPINION:

Flew the flag for Classic British Metal at a time when no-one but the fans really cared. Unfortunately, they continued to do the same after the fans stopped caring...

ACCEPTABLE CRITICISM:

Took Metal guitar into the '80s. And kept it there.

Metallica

HISTORY AND BACKGROUND:

Metallica have had more changes of staff than a blind knife-thrower, but unlike the ever-deteriorating **Deep Purple**, their current lineup (with twin guitarists James Hetfield and Kirk Hammett) is regarded as their best. Started early '80s as a Speed Metal act with obvious **NWOBHM** and **Motörhead** influences. Became the first US underground metal band to get a major label record deal. As albums developed, tempos dropped and production got slicker, but make no mistake - this band kicks ass. *Metallica* (known to fans as *The Black Album*) was their biggest-selling album to date, and stayed at the top of the US album charts for six weeks.

GUITARIST:

James Hetfield (vocal chords and power lines - or is it the other way round?) and Kirk Hammett (plays blues scales so fast that it sounds like he's almost happy).

GEAR:

Both play ESP signature guitars (Hetfield's is the copyright-infringingly-named 'Esplorer'), but for the late '90s albums *Load* and *Reload* they also used various vintage instruments, including a pedal steel Country guitar.

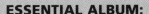

ESSENTIAL ALBUM:

The first one. Sure, *The Black Album* is a classic. *Master Of Puppets* broke them into popular appeal. But for sheer cool, you have to own the first Speed Metal album ever recorded - 1983's *Kill 'Em All* (if only because it was allegedly first titled *Metal Up Your Ass*).

FASCINATING FACT:

Their first album was allegedly first titled... oh, we've done that one, have we? How about the fact that they sacked guitarist Dave Mustaine in 1982, who went on to form **Megadeth**?... oh, so you already knew that, huh?

Well, I bet you didn't know about Apocolyptica? Ha! Got you. Apocalyptica are four 'cellists from Finland that recorded an album called *Metallica by Four Cellos*. Perhaps surprisingly, they never had quite the same success as the band themselves...

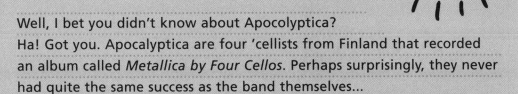

INSTANT OPINION:

"The most influential metal band of the 1980s, and still going strong."

ACCEPTABLE CRITICISM:

If you absolutely must criticise Metallica, show your devotion to 'true' metal by accusing them of 'selling out' (i.e. somebody bought their records) and 'being pop-metal wusses' (i.e. some of their songs had lyrics). And you could always disagree with Kirk's choice of eye-liner colour...

Emergency backup bluffs

Here are some bluffing basics on a further eight bands, just in case you need additional reference to prove your depth of knowledge.

1. Guns N' Roses

LA-based Hard Rock/Metal band formed in 1985. Guitarists Slash and Izzy Stradlin, both (mostly) Les Paul players. Massive albums including *Appetite For Destruction* and *Use Your Illusion I & II*. Slash is indirectly responsible for some of the most unpleasant sounds ever to come out of a guitar - not his own, I hasten to add - but take a trip to any guitar shop the world over and you'll hear some young guitar student almost, but not quite, completely failing to play the riff from 'Sweet Child O' Mine'.

2. Motörhead

Famously known as 'The Best Worst Band In The World', and proud of it. Centred around Brummie bassist Lemmy, and most notably featured Strat and Les Paul player 'Fast' Eddie Clarke. Tempos were ridiculous, vocals were yelled, lyrics were basic, and most fans were deaf. But they inspired Metallica and a whole load of other Speed/Punk/Thrash acts. And the rest is history.

3. Nirvana

Grunge, Punk, Metal, who cares what you call it? We're still talking great songs with attitude and noisy guitars, right? The tragically short-lived Nirvana started off playing lo-fi indie-rock, but got their big break with the classic '91 album *Nevermind* when singles such as 'Come As You Are' and 'Smells Like Teen Spirit' inspired (yet) another generation of wannabe rhythm guitar heroes. Kurt Cobain was the world's most celebrated user of the Fender 'Jag-stang' (a cross between a Jaguar and Mustang). He killed himself in 1994, but you can still hear his influence in tracks by PJ Harvey and Smashing Pumpkins.

4. Sepultura

You might think that the Brazilian Death/Thrash scene is not a big influence on metal today, but you'd be wrong. Sepultura combine traditional Brazilian folk music with blood-and-guts thrash to create some of the heaviest music ever to top the album charts. Yes, they are *that* successful. Originally the band went out with typical stage-names - Max Possessed, Tormentor, Destructor, and Igor Skull Crusher, though Tormentor was replaced by new guitar man Andreas Kisser (his real name, apparently). Guitar-vocalist Max Cavanera has recently departed to form Soulfly.

5. Red Hot Chili Peppers

Although this LA-based four-piece have tried their hands at a variety of rock styles, the one everyone seems to agree on is 'Funk Metal'. Guitarist Dave Navarro (ex-Jane's Addiction - Strats and Marshalls) was with them during their most successful period. Bassist Flea was also a big influence on many - he managed to make slap bass playing socially acceptable for a brief period (and a brief period of slap bass playing is all most of us can stand anyway). Album to own is 1993's *BloodSugarSexMagik*, with big singles 'Give It Away' and 'Under The Bridge'.

6. Pantera

Playing just on the edge of what most old-style metal fans find listenable, Pantera are variously identified as Power Metal, Glam-rock, Speed Metal or Thrash, depending on which album you listen to. Started life as a Glam band in the vein of Kiss, but soon settled into heavier (and more cred-worthy) territory. Guitarist 'Dimebag Darrell' is a Washburn endorsee - you can get his distinctive Explorer-style signature guitar in a variety of finishes, including 'Dime Slime'. Breakthrough album *Far Beyond Driven* is typical '90s metal - double bass-drumming, tight rhythm playing and growly vocals. Hint - most young Pantera fans don't know about their heroes' shady past. Hours of fun can be had showing them pictures of the band from 1988. Rumour has it that the band had these early photos destroyed.

7. Green Day

Strictly speaking, this is more Punk than metal, but if we're defining Heavy Metal as 'that-which-may-appear-on-the-cover-of-*Kerrang*', then Green Day are definitely allowed in this book. Guitar-vocalist Billie Joe Armstrong (customised Strat) formed his first band with bassist Mike Dirnt when they were 14 - drummer Tre Cool joined Green Day shortly after their first album. Considering their Punk mentality, they actually whack out some amazingly tuneful songs (so much so that they get MTV airplay, and their tracks appear in US TV shows such as ER and Seinfeld). There's very little flash guitar playing and hardly any solos, but this is still '90s Alternative Metal at its best.

8. The Instrumentalists

Instrumental metal is hardly the coolest thing right now - you certainly never hear it in the charts - but it's probably a bigger influence on guitarists than any other form. Between the mid-80s and early '90s, players wanted to learn

every hammer-on, pick-scrape and fret-buzz from their heroes. Of the big names - Joe Satriani, Steve Vai, Jennifer Batten, Vinnie Moore and Yngwie Malmsteen (who usually hired in a vocalist, but the albums were still really extended solos!) - Satriani and Vai are the two most significant. Satch is usually associated with melodic, smooth-toned tracks with a fairly straightforward backing - the virtuoso stuff is all in the playing. With Vai, pretty much anything goes - he's taken instrumental guitar music to ridiculous extremes, and is thought by many to be the world's greatest living guitar player. Just remember - the definition of a true gentleman is someone who can play instrumental metal... and doesn't.

It's Easy To Bluff...
Music and TAB Guide

Most guitar players can't read music. There. We've said it. So you can stop feeling guilty about it and get on with the serious business of pretending that you can. On these two pages you'll find tab and treble clef notation for all of the techniques featured in this book, along with tips on how to play them.

HOW TO READ TREBLE CLEF: The note on the bottom line of the treble clef is middle E - that is, it's the E which is found on the 2nd fret of the D string. The top line is F (1st fret, high E string).

Guitar notes that are lower or higher than this range are notated using 'leger lines' - these are extra stave lines drawn in above or below the main clef.

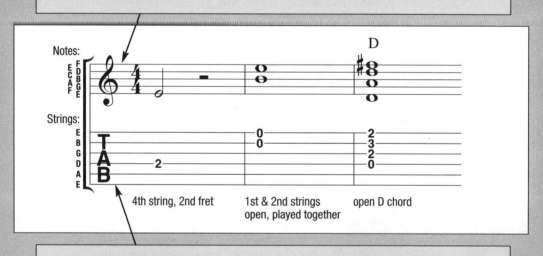

4th string, 2nd fret   1st & 2nd strings open, played together   open D chord

HOW TO READ TAB: The six lines represent the strings - the thickest (lowest) string is at the bottom. The number shows the fret.

HOW TO READ CHORD PARTS: The chord names are written above, and sometimes the musical rhythm of the part is notated underneath.

If no rhythm is given, or you see several even 'slashes' in a bar, then normally you should make up your own rhythm pattern. If you see two chords in a bar, it's normally assumed that they're played for two beats each.

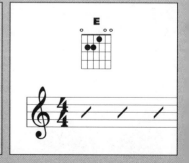

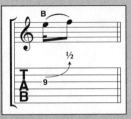

SEMITONE BEND (OR HALF-STEP BEND): Play the note with the picking hand then bend it up a semitone (so it reaches the pitch of the note on the next fret).

WHOLE TONE BEND: Duh! Just bend it further!

PICK SCRAPE: Rub the edge of the pick down (or up) the string, to produce a scratchy, 'heavy' sound.

QUARTER-TONE BEND: Just bend the string a little - don't go as far as a semitone. Quarter-tone is used to mean any bend that's less than a semitone.

BEND AND RELEASE: Play the note, bend it up, let it back down again.

PRE-BEND: Bend the note up before you play it.

PRE-BEND AND RELEASE: Bend the note up, then play it, then release the bend while the note rings on.

VIBRATO: Move the string up and down by rapidly bending and releasing it by a small amount.

HAMMER-ON: Pick one note, then sound the higher note by fretting it without re-picking. Hammer-ons are always ascending in pitch.

PULL-OFF: Get both fingers into the positions shown in the tab, then pick the higher note. Whilst it rings on, pull the finger off the string to sound the lower note.

SLIDE/GLISS: While the note is sounding, slide the fretting finger up or down to the position shown in the tab.

SLIDE/GLISS AND RESTRIKE: As before, but this time repick the second note after you've finishing sliding.

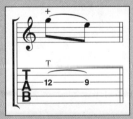

TAPPING: Fret the note using the picking hand by tapping onto the position shown. Usually followed by a pull-off.

PALM MUTING: Rest the picking hand on the strings very near to the bridge. This partially mutes the notes - the technique is used a lot in blues and rock rhythm playing.

SLASH CHORDS: Many players get confused when they see chord notation like this for the first time. Do not fear - it's simple. The letter name before the slash is the chord you play. The one after the slash is the bass note. Bluffing tip - if you find it too difficult to play a particular bass note at the same time as the chord, try ignoring it and just playing the chord, then get a bassist or keyboard player to supply the bottom end.

Angus Young in full flow, just before he rushes off for his oxygen fix.

Rhythm Patterns or 'Get Your Motor Runnin''

If you have to bluff your way through a whole metal gig, you'll need to convince everyone in the band that you know your 'rhythm chops', so it's vital that you can play some basic accompaniment styles.

In this section you'll find 10 rhythm and picking patterns, in progressive order of difficulty, that guitarists use when playing in a band context under a singer or lead player.

Rhythm Tips

- **Use a plectrum. Always. Most players opt for a thick one - 1mm or more.**
- Rest the picking-hand palm gently on the strings near the bridge to create palm-mutes, then use eight-to-the-bar downstrokes with the plectrum. If you're playing Speed Metal, you need to be able to play eighth notes at around 180BPM (check out Metallica's Master Of Puppets - yep, it's downstrokes all the way!)
- **Power chords only. Don't wuss about with Sus 4s, minor 9ths etc. Even 7ths will make you sound like a blues band.**
- There's a common misconception that the more distortion you use, the heavier it will sound. This is rarely true, because if you bury the whole mix in distortion, the attack of the chord is lost, so the whole mix doesn't 'rock'.
- **Don't strum all six strings, all the time. Most rhythm parts only use two or three bass strings.**
- Experiment with tunings. Many players (Cobain, Hendrix) dropped the whole guitar by a semitone. Heavier bands use dropped tunings (dropping the bass string, usually down to D). *Really* heavy guitar bands drop the tunings even further - e.g. Korn use 7-string Ibanez Universe guitars, with the bottom string tuned to A.
- **Add a short delay to the sound to simulate doubled rhythm tracks...**
- ...or if you're recording, try double-tracking the rhythm part. Skunk Anansie, Pantera and Rage Against The Machine frequently do this.
- **Accent certain beats in the bar. This is vital to avoid your eighth notes sounding boring, and is standard practice in Thrash and Speed Metal.**
- Make sure you mute *every* string you're not using. Unwanted open strings can completely kill a rhythm part.

'Palm Sabbath'

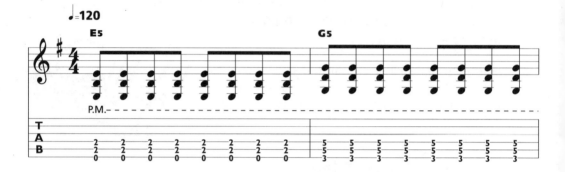

This riff makes use of one of the most important skills in a Metal player's arsenal - palm muting.

You can vary the effect by positioning your picking hand closer to or further away from the bridge. Use lots of bass end and a surprisingly small amount of distortion to rattle the glasses from the tables!

'Maiden Punch'

Beloved of **Iron Maiden** among others, this idea features contrasting palm mutes and insistent chord stabs, which are mostly ahead of the beat, giving more 'punch'.

 # Handy Hint

> Feet should be wide apart, with the guitar facing approx. 180° from the torso.

'Reinforced Wrist'

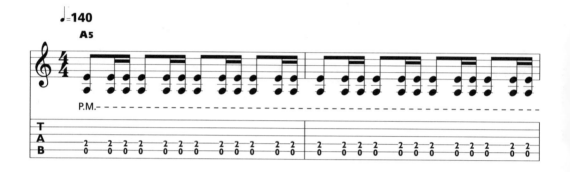

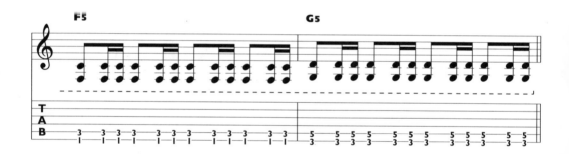

A classic 'galloping' rhythm, very popular during the resurgence of Metal in the early '80s.

The tempos for this kind of track tend to be fairly high, so keep your picking hand wrist as relaxed as possible, or a five minute song could leave you gasping for air.

Perhaps a sports wrist support underneath the studded leather one would be in order!

'Rhythmic Surprise'

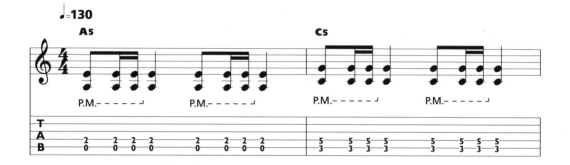

Mixing the galloping idea with chord stabs gives the best of both worlds. Shake the walls with some palm muted power chords, then let rip with a ringing one over and over again.

It at any time you feel the rhythm is becoming predictable, or you just want to give people a surprise, try a variation like the one in the last bar.

'Motöring Both Ways'

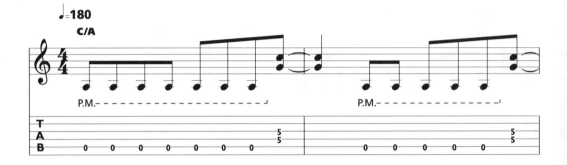

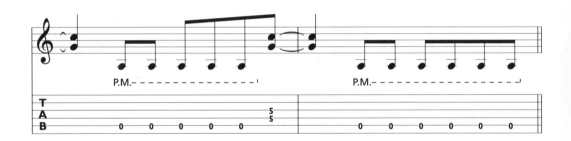

Moving further uptempo, bands like **AC/DC** and **Motörhead** have made great use of this rhythmic device, using the ever-present palm muting and chord stabs 'on a push'.

 # Handy Hint

Make the most of these stabs by making sure the muting is precise and thorough. Naturally, all the muted notes should be played on a downstroke (upstrokes being for cheats and wusses, as we know).

'Spaced Cowboy'

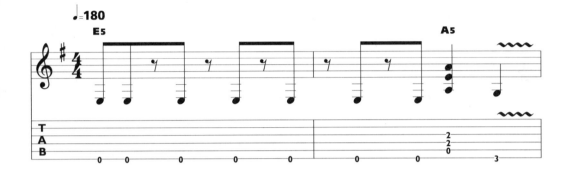

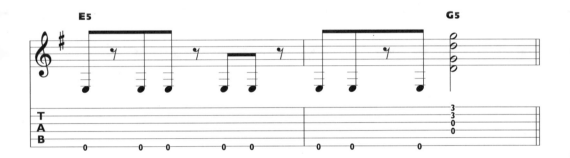

Used by **Pantera**'s Dimebag Darrell on 'Cowboys From Hell', this technique requires super accurate muting, to ensure the rest spaces are absolutely noise-free.

Avoiding any echo or reverb effects beyond an optional short delay.

'Bouncing Metal'

You'll hear this lively '90s Metal rhythm on **Metallica**'s 'Don't Tread On Me', and with a slight twist on **The Red Hot Chili Peppers**' version of 'Higher Ground'. Make sure the muted bass notes don't 'bleed' into the chords or you'll lose power.

This idea blends well with fast thrash workouts too when played by the likes of **Slayer** or **Sepultura**.

'Turn Up The Contrast'

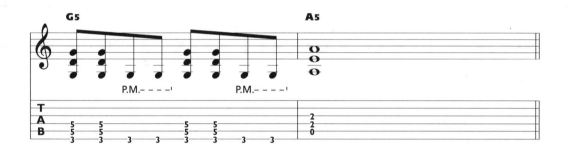

This aggressive rhythm uses the full force of the power chord, followed by a more restrained palm mute on the root note. The key element once again is contrast, otherwise the listener will not appreciate how magnificently powerful your tone really is.

 Push It Further!

To push those accents further, a little co-operation from the bass player and drummer will also do no harm.

'Heavy Tone'

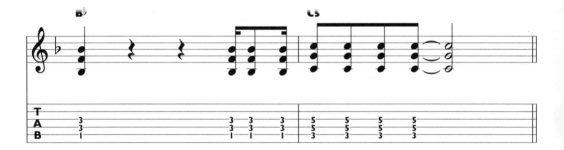

Think of **The Cult**, **Judas Priest** or **AC/DC** and you won't go far wrong with this pattern, whatever chords you choose to play.

Like most rhythmic patterns in Metal, open chords are avoided - well, apart from E. The idea is that a thicker string fretted higher gives a heavier sound. (To check this out, play the third string open, then the fifth string at the 10th fret. Both positions give the same note but a vastly different tone.)

'Live On Arrival'

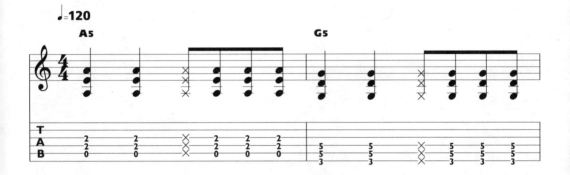

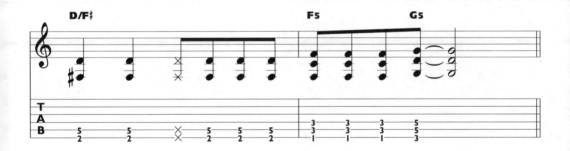

Sometimes it's OK to use 'deliberately messy' string noise.

This example is reminiscent of **Van Halen**'s 'D.O.A.' Juggle the rhythm around a little and you have the basis of **Nirvana**'s 'Smells Like Teen Spirit'. This kind of percussive effect is also very popular with the Funk Metal fraternity.

Metallica's **Kirk Hammett** - master of riffery.

Riffs and Licks or 'Play it over and over until it sounds good'

Metal wouldn't have got anywhere without the guitar riff.
Try to imagine 'Paranoid' without that classic hammer-on intro,
or 'Ain't Talkin' 'Bout Love' without that picked A minor chord.
And the strange thing about most riffs is - they're so simple,
you can't believe you didn't write them yourself.

What's a riff?

A riff is a short guitar phrase, almost always one, two or four bars in length,
which repeats at various points throughout the track. It can be transposed (moving
into different fingerboard positions when the chords change) or it may be slightly
modified to take account of the changes.

What's a lick?

In this section, we've also included 'licks'. A lick is a lead guitar part that
you learn beforehand, and then include as part of a so-called 'improvised' solo.
It follows that licks are, of course, vital to a bluffer's defensive equipment, because
they can be inserted in a lead part without anyone knowing that you prepared
them before the gig.

JARGON

The difference between a riff and a lick is basically that
you may only use a lick once (pretending it's a great phrase
you just thought up) but you can use a riff over and over (demonstrating
how you can make one simple idea into a whole musical experience).

In this section you'll find riffs and licks of varying levels of difficulty, together with
tips and suggestions about when - and when not - to use them. If you're a complete
beginner on guitar, don't be afraid to concentrate purely on the easy examples -
some of them look more difficult than they actually are.

'Five-key Fretwork'

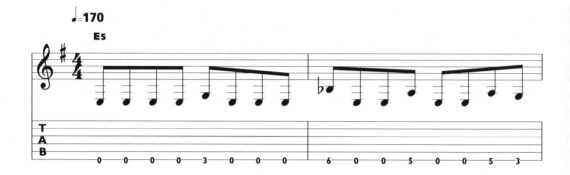

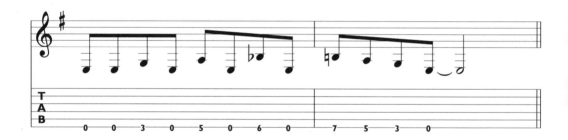

This riff demonstrates how Metal guitarists often explore the melodic and tonal possibilities of a single string.

 Using open notes between melody notes can add power and depth to a phrase (e.g. the guitar intro on **Iron Maiden**'s 'Wasted Years'). This is ideal for bluffing, as you know it will work in the keys of E, A, D, G, or B!

'Rapid Fire'

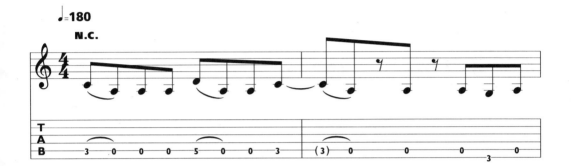

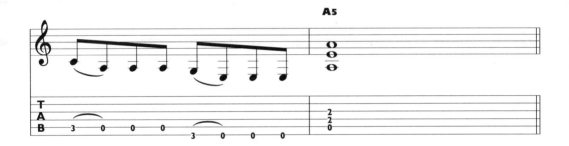

Using single notes and bursts of silence, this example features the kind of techniques used currently by **Korn** (e.g. 'Justin'). Adding a phase, wah, or flange effect takes you into the territory of modern Metal, convincing all onlookers that you must really have your finger on the pulse.

It's also effective if you tune your guitar way below concert pitch.

'Heavy Love Night'

This riff is in the key of F#, cited by **Pantera**'s Dimebag as "one of the heaviest keys of all time", and featured on their track 'This Love'.
A similar chord movement can be heard on
Whitesnake's undeniably heavy 'Still Of The Night'.

The chord movements here are quick
enough to imply a melody, which
is perhaps the ultimate
definition of a rhythm riff.

'Speed Demon'

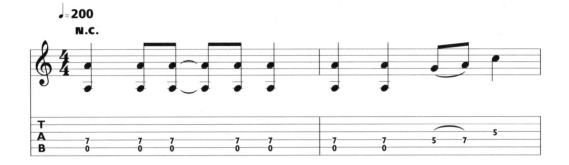

Played mostly in octaves, this example is from the same stable as **Motörhead**'s 'Ace Of Spades'. Though the original riff was actually played on bass, it transfers well to guitar and this variation will help display your thorough knowledge of this style.

 **Handy Hint**

> Ignore all the usual guitar-teacher advice about minimum movement in the picking hand and get your whole arm going!

'Make War Not Love'

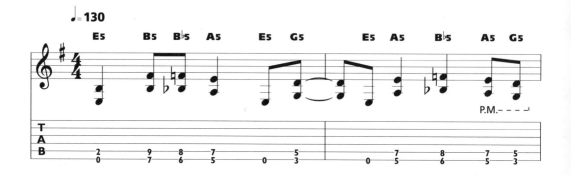

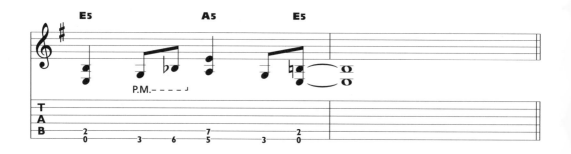

Using lots of very menacing sounding B♭ chords, this example draws from **Black Sabbath**'s 'War Pigs', **Megadeth**'s 'Holy Wars', and **Slayer**'s 'War Ensemble'.

Note the 'War' connection; anything dramatic or disastrous usually features lots of E and B♭ freely mixed.

'Naked Rage'

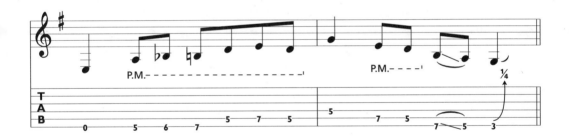

This fast-moving example is based around the E blues scale; E, G, A, B♭, B, D -
it's the kind of riff featured in **Reef**'s 'Naked', or even **Rage Against The
Machine**'s 'Killing In The Name'.

Using the bridge pickup will give a more 'traditional' Metal tone, but changing
to a single-coil neck pickup will give you a more funky sound. **Oh, and wear your
baseball cap back to front.**

'War Chimes'

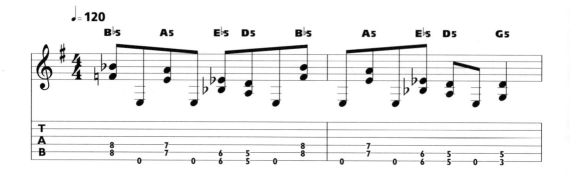

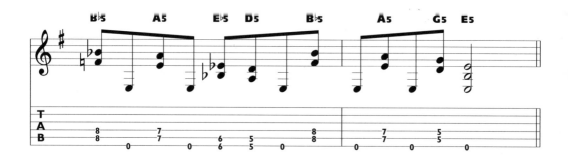

This **Slayer**-style riff further proves the mystic connection between ♭5 chord progressions and songs with 'War' in the title. Boost the bass and treble on your amp or pedals, while turning the midrange right down or even off.

'Riff Bloody Riff'

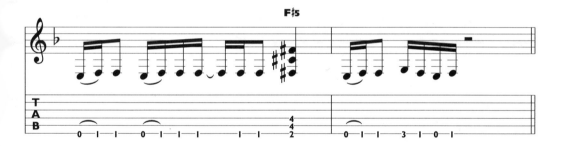

Using chords you might not expect to play in the key of F, this riff mixes single notes and power chord stabs in a style similar to **Sepultura**'s 'Roots Bloody Roots'.

If you get the chance to play this with another guitarist, get him/her to play just the power chord stabs for maximum heaviness. If you are playing alone, simply make sure you hit them hard (the chords, not the other guitarist).

'Machine Gun Metal'

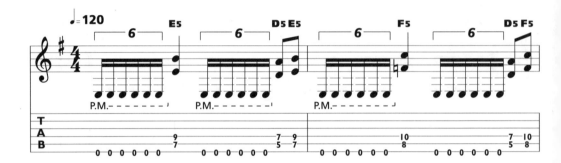

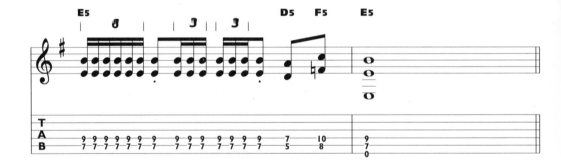

A challenging sextuplet pattern on the sixth string gives way to no-holds-barred power chord accents. This is one of the rare occasions where it is not only permissible, but necessary to use alternate down/upstrokes for a Metal rhythm riff.

To hear this idea in use, check out the ending of **Metallica**'s 'One'.

'Crazy Oz'

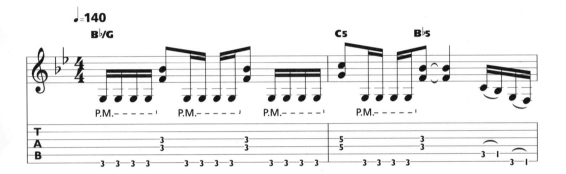

A tricky pattern, again using alternate picking for the muted semiquaver root notes.

This style calls to mind **Ozzy Osborne**'s 'I Don't Know' or 'Shot In The Dark' among others. The most important elements of this technique are to keep the tempo even, while making sure those bass notes are firmly under control. **Great for Intros, or unaccompanied music shop riffing.**

'Moore Speed'

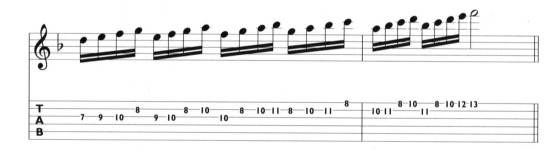

This one's a great technique building exercise, often used by **Gary Moore** in his pre-Blues days on tracks like *Out In The Fields*.

Start this one slowly and build up gradually to breakneck speed! A little palm muting on the lower notes may prove handy if you are playing at high volume or with lots of distortion (ideally both!) Use alternate picking throughout, starting on a downstroke.

Less Haste, **Moore** Speed!

'Throw Away Your Pick'

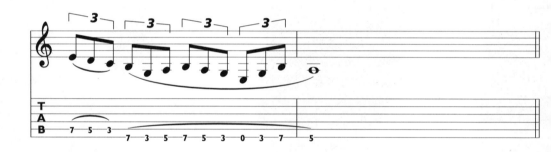

If alternate picking seems a bit too much like hard work, try this legato run using hammer-ons and pull-offs.

Featuring prominently in the recordings of **Joe Satriani** and **Steve Vai**, this technique gives a more fluent, relaxed effect than fast picking. It also means you can give your picking arm a rest without having to stop 'ripping it up'. **If your fretting hand is strong enough, this can be played without any picking at all.**

'Pick It Up Again'

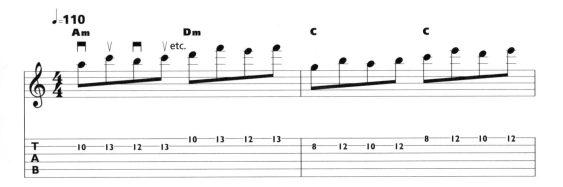

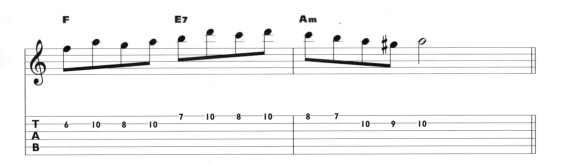

Here is a neo-classical style descending run in the style of **Randy Rhoads** or **Yngwie Malmsteen**. Using alternate picking, this run can be played anywhere on the neck with little modification.

 **Take Note!**

As with all speed techniques, build up slowly and carefully until you can dash it off without so much as a second glance at the fretboard!

'Harmonic Metal'

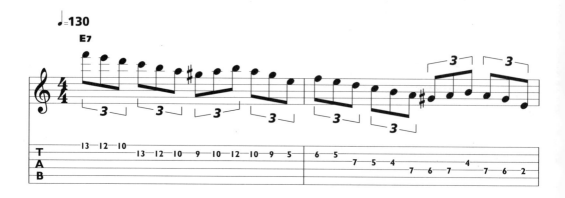

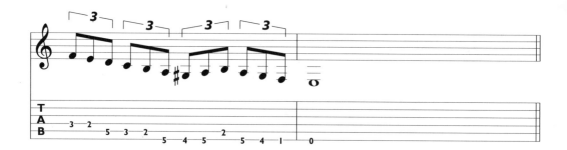

No Metal book would be complete without at least one example of the Harmonic Minor scale. This phrase is based in the key of A, but is designed to be played over a hanging E or E7 chord, before the magnificent return to the home key.

Choose your fingering positions carefully, bearing in mind some of the huge position jumps, which are probably easiest using the first finger.

'Stock Soulful Lick'

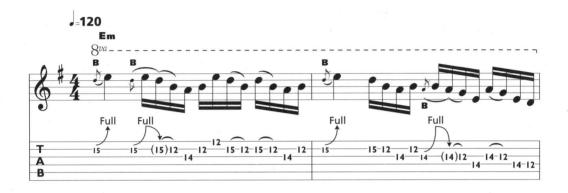

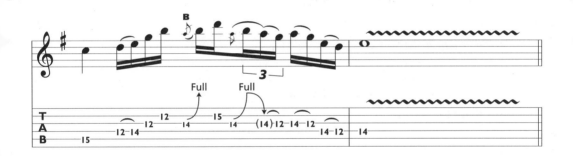

This blues-based phrase features string bends, pull offs and vibrato. Every Metal lead player has a few 'stock' licks like this, from **Slash** to **Kirk Hammett**. In the middle of a raging thrash song, this soulful kind of playing really stands out.

Add a long reverb or delay, and the scenario is complete. Try varying with the speed of bends and vibrato.

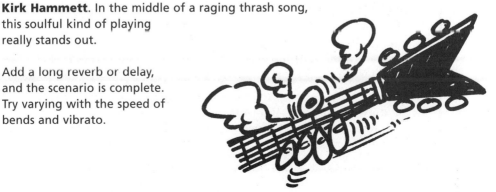

Specialist Techniques or 'But I've Only Got Ten Fingers...'

Sometimes it's not enough to learn all the notes of the fingerboard, then every chord and scale you're ever likely to need. Unfortunately, there are difficult techniques to master too.

However, don't worry - in Metal there are only half a dozen or so, and this section shows you all you need to convince every audience member that you're a true specialist. Here, we've covered five techniques - tapping, whammy-bar tricks, sweep-picking, palm harmonics and multi-finger tapping. These are not selected because they're the most musically valid or even the best-sounding. They're just the best ones for showing off.

 ## Six Top Tricks

- **PINCHED HARMONICS:** Those 'squealy' noises a lead player makes. Created by digging in to the string with the side of the thumb as you pick the note with a plectrum. Sounds fantastic, though it can be overused by some. Needs a high-gain, heavily distorted sound.

- **GARGLING:** Play a note, flick the whammy bar so it goes 'boing'. Stupidly easy and sounds incredible. **Van Halen** and **Extreme** were keen on it in the early '90s. Out of favour with most Nu-Metal acts now.

- **DROPPED TUNINGS:** Just detune the whole guitar by a semitone or several for a REALLY heavy sound. **Korn**, **Pantera**, **Soulfly**, **Kurt Cobain**, and **Jimi Hendrix** can't all be wrong, can they?

- **CONTROLLED FEEDBACK:** Sound a note with amp distortion on it, then walk up to a LOUD amp. The amp drives the air, the air vibrates and drives the string, the string vibrates and you hear it through the amp. Bonus points if you can do it while waggling your tongue at the audience.

- **DELAYS:** Most famously used by Nuno Bettencourt in **Extreme**'s 'Flight of the Wounded Bumble Bee'. Set a delay line so a single note is repeated slightly slower than your picking speed. If you can get the picking speed *exactly* two thirds of the delay time, you create this illusion that you can play twice as fast as you really can. Difficult but (some say) worth the effort.

- **DIVE BOMBS:** Basically, playing a note then pushing the whammy bar down all the way. Also works with some types of harmonic. AKA 'Motorbike' noises. Again, very 'Eighties', but great fun, and worth buying a Superstrat for.

'Skipping Triplet Taps'

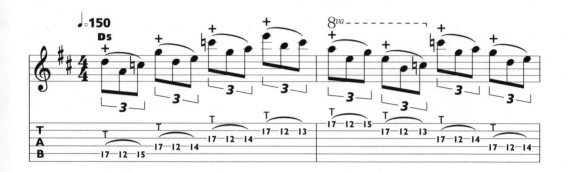

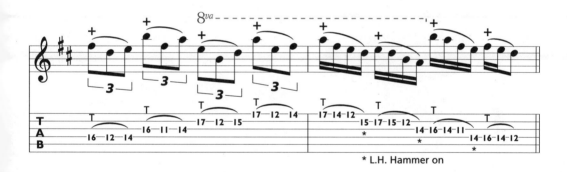

* L.H. Hammer on

Tapping Lick 1.

Mixing a few different tapping ideas, this phrase is similar to some of Nuno Bottencourt's work with **Extremo**. Based around C major then D major arpeggios, the faster you can play this the better!

The last bar of semiquavers sounds very impressive when it kicks in, so it's worth spending some time to get it really accurate.

Edward Van Halen - did he invent tapping or didn't he?

'Vesuvian'

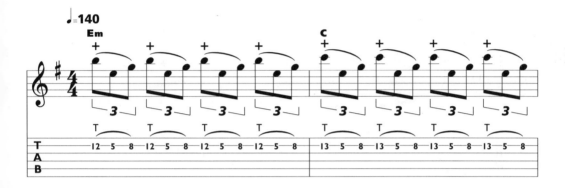

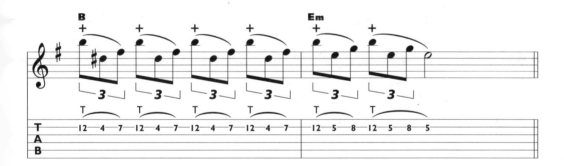

Tapping Lick 2.

This is the technique used by **Eddie Van Halen** in his solo guitar masterpiece 'Eruption'. To help with articulation, pull your tapping finger upwards, rather than just lifting it off.

When you have this down, try swapping around the order of the nontapped notes e.g. in the first bar, try B, G, E, instead of B, E, G. Even if this is done at random, the results can be very impressive...

'Never-Ending Tap'

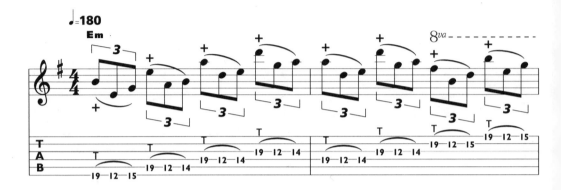

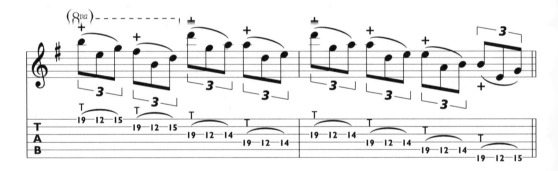

Tapping Lick 3.

Here's a deceptively simple tapping phrase, based around the E minor pentatonic scale, with all the taps occurring at the 19th fret.

Again, there are hundreds of possibilities for juggling around the notes, meaning it is feasible to keep this going for quite some time without it becoming too repetitive. **Ideal for getting you through a difficult solo.**

'Diving Without Air'

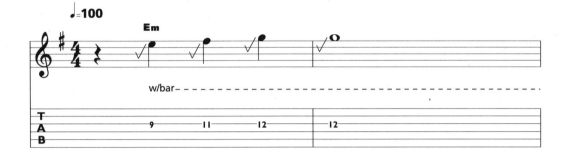

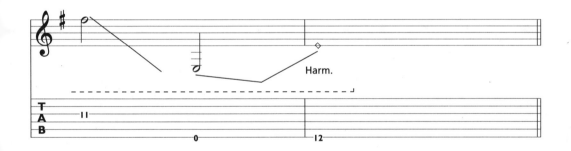

Whammy Bar Madness 1.

Time to push your strings to their limit! This example showcases a couple of ways you can use the tremolo for anything but tasteful vibrato. The 'scoops' in the first bar actually dispense with the need for picking.

The 'divebombs' speak for themselves, though the last bar demonstrates how you can touch on a harmonic while the strings are almost slack, and give your listeners a surprise when the note comes back up to pitch.

'Gargling'

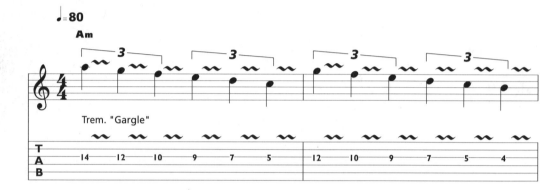

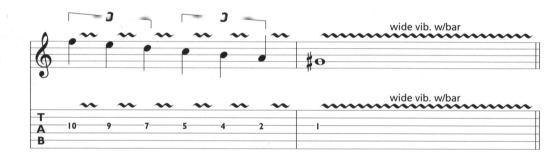

Whammy Bar Madness 2.

This technique is prominently used by players like **Joe Satriani** and **Steve Vai**. It involves 'pinging' the end of the bar, so the string goes 'boing!'.

The best results are achieved with a locking vibrato system, but it is also possible with a 'vintage' style unit, as long as you have it set with some upward travel.

Joe 'Satch' Satriani. Spends more time at the bar than an alcoholic barrister.

'Small Sweeps'

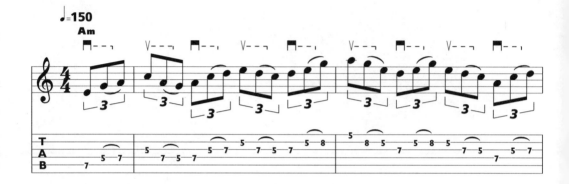

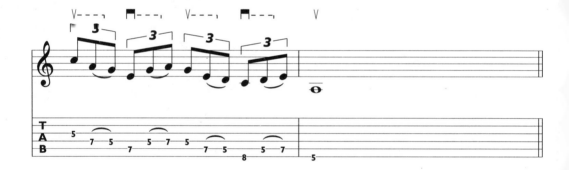

Sweep Picking 1.

Sweep-picking is the technique of picking in one direction at a time, and fretting the notes briefly as you play them (picking directions given on the tab). Like tapping, it means you can play wide intervals at high speed.

Though most people associate sweep picking with **Yngwie Malmsteen** and speed-of-light arpeggios, it has a few other tricks up its sleeve too. This pentatonic **Gary Moore**-style run uses a small sweeping motion to add speed and fluency when moving across the strings. This is a useful introduction to the principles of this technique, which can be adapted in various ways.

'Sweeping All The Way'

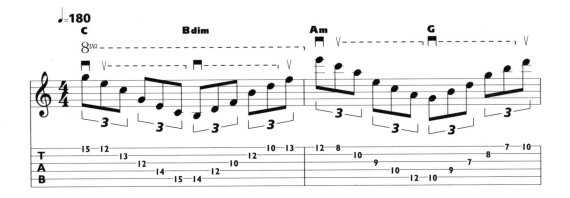

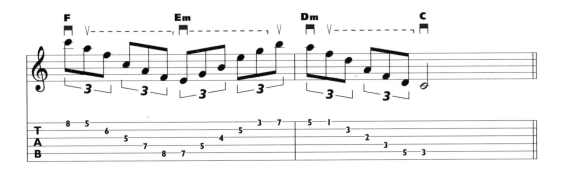

Sweep Picking 2.

Because it uses several arpeggio ideas, this sweep picking frenzy will require some patient practice, though when your fretting hand has learned the positions, you are in for a pleasant surprise.

Though this kind of playing sounds absolutely blistering, there is not as much physical effort required as for alternate picking. This is more of a 'knack'.

'Palm Harmonics'

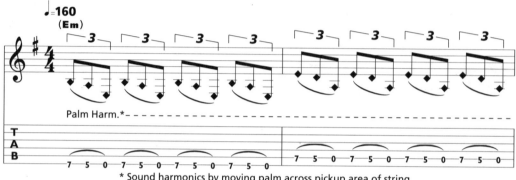

* Sound harmonics by moving palm across pickup area of string

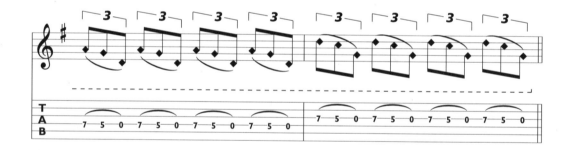

Dial in the dirtiest sound you can, then sound these notes as fast as you can with your fretting hand, while moving the palm of your picking hand along the strings over the pickups.

There is no need to pick anything, just keep your palm moving to sound amazing random harmonics. **Eddie Van Halen** uses this technique on the track 'Somebody Get Me A Doctor'.

'Six-Finger Tapping'

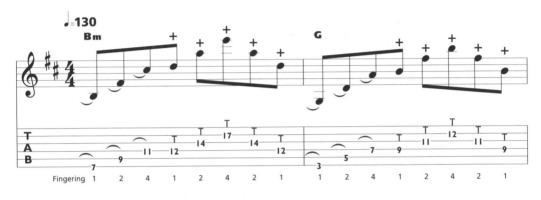

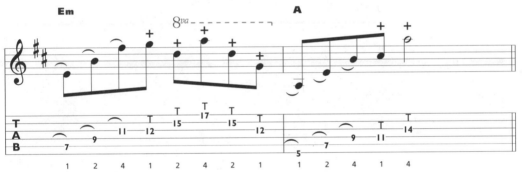

As if tapping with one finger was not enough, try this phrase arranged for six. The first three notes of each bar are sounded by simply hammering on with the fretting hand.

The remaining five are tapped with the fingers of your picking hand, which looks pretty impressive. Which fingers you use is a matter of experimentation, though resting your thumb on the neck helps this technique feel more comfortable.

Specialist Metal or
'How To Survive The Rock Bore'

If you've read this far, your bluffing skills will be almost foolproof. Almost. There are certain musical styles that attract such loyal devotees that a mere smattering of knowledge is not enough for the would-be Metal-meister.

In this section, we've given some musical examples that are particular to three specific types - Punk, Thrash and Funk Metal. These are the styles you need to have - literally - at your fingertips if your metallic credibility is doubted.

Long curly perm and grimace
are obviously crucial

For each style, three riffs or licks are supplied - this is the number you'll need before you can drag the conversation round to a style you *do* know something about.

'Barre Chord Kicks'

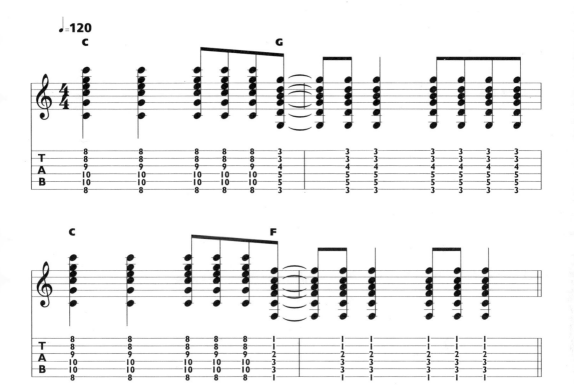

Punk 1.

One of the main differences between Punk and other forms of Metal is the approach to chords. Traditional Metal players tend to avoid having more than three notes ringing at once - and one of those is usually the octave of the root note.

Punk players often go for a full major bar chord and strum it with gusto on all six strings. A good example of this is the **Undertones'** rhythm guitar parts, though you'll have heard it more recently on **Green Day** and **Smashing Pumpkins** albums.

'Are You Calling Me A Wimp?'

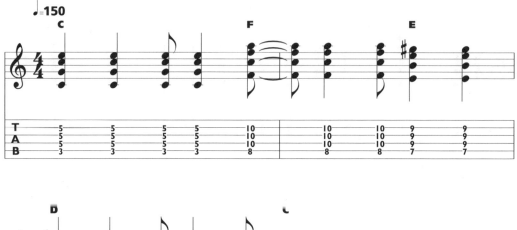

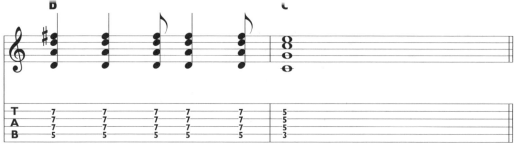

Punk 2.

This slightly smaller four-string barre shape was very popular with the **Sex Pistols**, and can be heard on the track 'Holiday In The Sun'. Note how the movement to E major in the second bar doesn't really fit. This is partially covered by the distortion, and partly by the attitude **"This Is Punk And I Don't Give A S**t"**.

'Wanna Make Something Of It?'

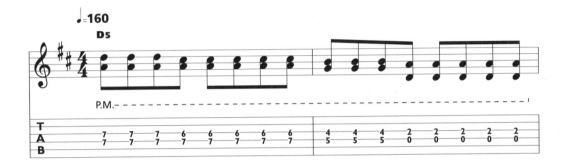

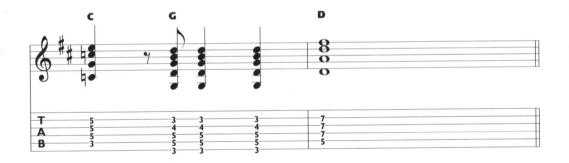

Punk 3.

Here's an even more aggressive punk riff, which combines with explosive power chords in a style similar to the **Skids**' 'Into The Valley'.

With obviously Metal roots, the major barre chords add a primitive edge, which complements the low-fi buzzy distortion many of these guitarists used.

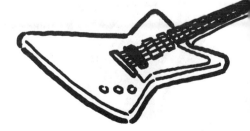

'Testament To Triplets'

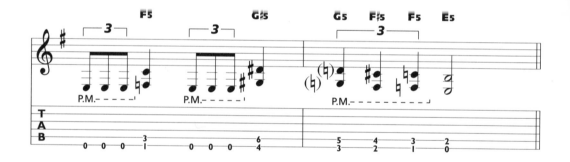

Thrash 1.

This is a trademark thrash riff, in the style of **Metallica** or **Testament**. The chord movements are strange and dramatic, but keep within the stripped-down power chord framework.

Make sure you have the bridge pickup selected, with little or no midrange at the amplifier, but lots of everything else!

'Stab In The Darkness'

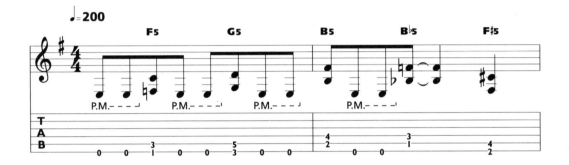

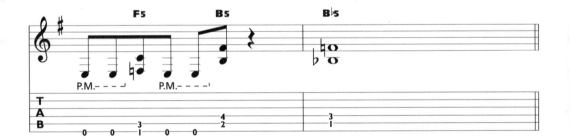

Thrash 2.

Using a muted open E bass note, the chords in this example appear as dramatic stabs. Lots of semitone chord shifts are a classic Thrash technique, as is the use of a B♭ chord both during the riff and for its finale.

The tempo here is just a guide, as of course you should be aiming to play these riffs as fast as you possibly can.

'Slow Deth'

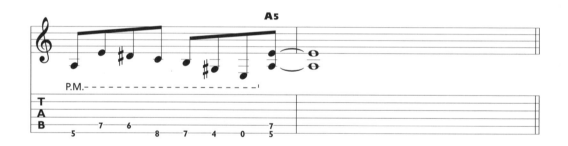

Thrash 3.

Mixing chord stabs and single notes in the style of **Slayer** or **Megadeth**, this example could be played on two guitars in unison or with one just doubling up on the accents.

The palm muting should be relatively light, so that the bass notes are punchy and controlled, but not too staccato.

'Jimi's Angry'

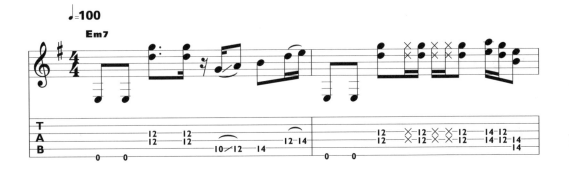

Funk 1.

A busy, funky riff, split into bass and chord parts, this example stands up well even unaccompanied. The trick to making a part like this groove is to exaggerate everything about it, from the intensity of accents (wherever you decide to put them) to the percussive string noises.

Think of **Hendrix** jamming with **Rage Against The Machine**!

'Dead On The Groove'

Funk 2.

This example takes inspiration from the **Red Hot Chili Peppers**' 'Give It Away', and should also be played with a fairly heavy handed but precise touch.

The amount of distortion is not as crucial as it would be for an out-and-out power chord riff, but you will need plenty of treble.

'Funked Up The Mix'

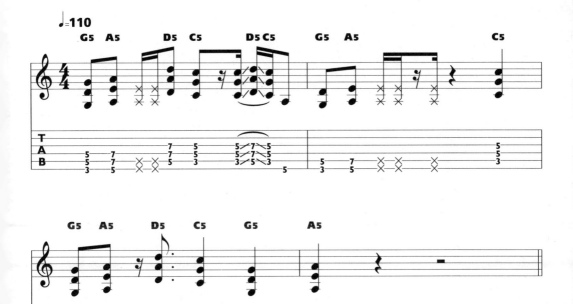

Funk 3.

Combining a bit of **Faith No More** with elements of **Reef** and just plain ol' Classic Metal can give a result like this. Again, keep distortion levels lower than you might for a Thrash riff, preserving a few more of the dynamics of your picking attack.

Faith No More - Funk Not Metal?

Music Shop Classic or 'How do I fit everything in this book into two minutes of showing off?'

This custom-designed showpiece should amaze any onlookers and cynical staff at your local guitar shop. It's been specially devised to be utterly without the shackles of musical subtlety, emotional validity or artistic good taste. It's all here - from pick scrapes and heavy power chords, to wailing bends at the top of the fretboard, with lots of envy-inducing tricks in between.

Before you venture into the guitar shop to impress everyone, make sure you have warmed up thoroughly at home, though it will do no harm to mutter something like 'Wow, I haven't played for ages', as you plug in.

Make sure you have a great tone set on the amp before you start, play the piece through until jaws are dropping, then put on a worried frown as you adjust the treble by 1000th of a millimetre. Then play the whole thing again...

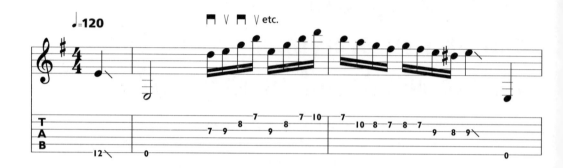

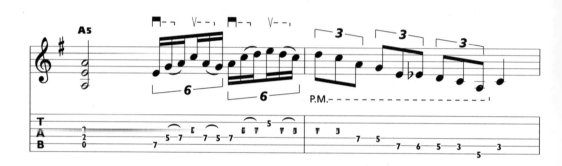

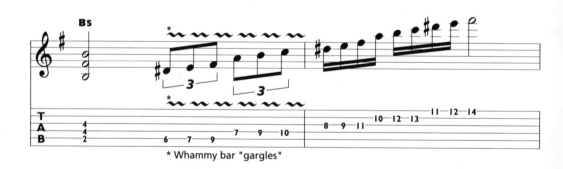

* Whammy bar "gargles"

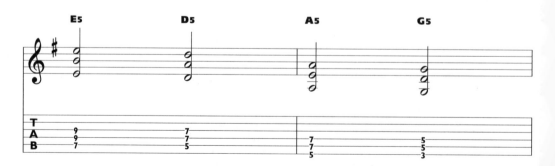

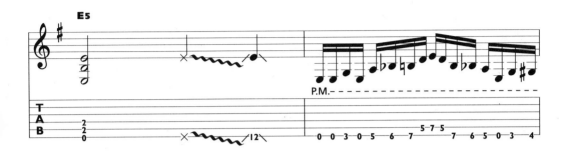

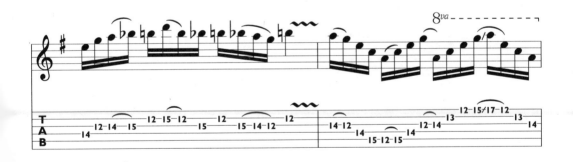

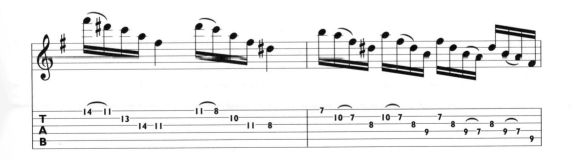

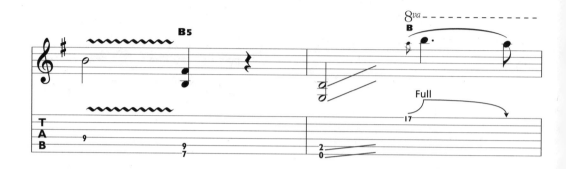

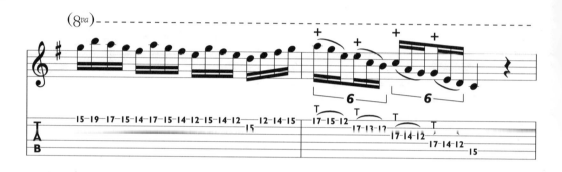

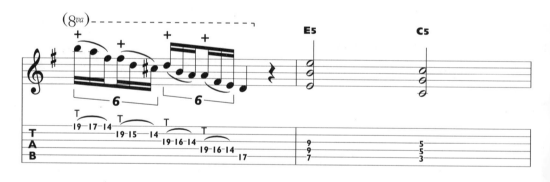

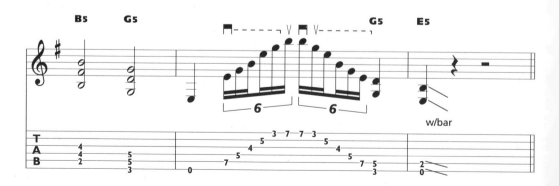

Guitar Sounds or 'Who Cares How It Sounds When It's This Loud?'

Players often convince themselves that they need the exact same gear as their heroes before they can create convincing sounds. In fact, with a guitar that plays in tune, a reliable amp, and a selection of effects, you can get a useable version of every Metal tone you ever wanted.

On these pages, we've shown diagrams of a typical pedals setup for five basic sounds. (Note - multi-FX owners should assume that all values are out of 10, except for delay times - our delay pedal shown has a maximum time setting of 1000ms, so if the dial's at 12 o'clock, that means a 500ms, or half-second delay).

Blues-Rock Setup

Use middle pickup

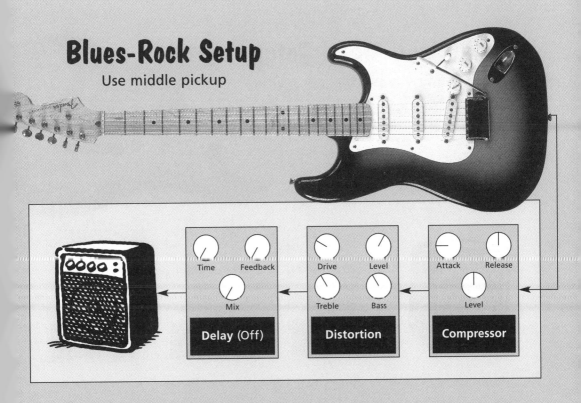

Time Feedback

Mix

Delay (Off)

Drive Level

Treble Bass

Distortion

Attack Release

Level

Compressor

Classic Metal Setup

Use bridge pickup

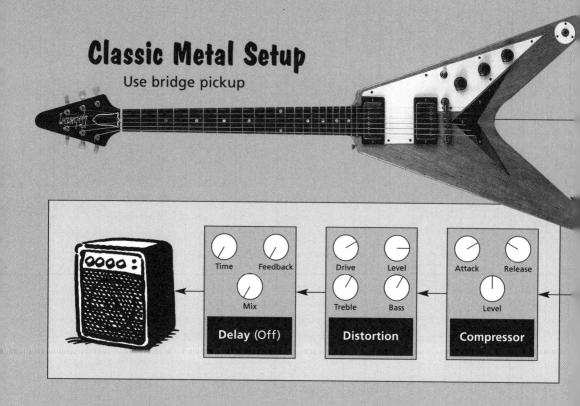

| Time | Feedback |
| Mix |
| **Delay (Off)** |

| Drive | Level |
| Treble | Bass |
| **Distortion** |

| Attack | Release |
| Level |
| **Compressor** |

American Metal Setup

Use bridge pickup

| Time | Feedback |
| Mix |
| **Delay** |

| Drive | Level |
| Treble | Bass |
| **Distortion** |

| Attack | Release |
| Level |
| **Compressor** |

Thrash Setup
Use bridge pickup

Delay	Distortion	Compressor
Time, Feedback, Mix	Drive, Level, Treble, Bass	Attack, Release, Level

Funk Metal Setup
Use both pickups

Delay (Off)	Distortion	Compressor
Time, Feedback, Mix	Drive, Level, Treble, Bass	Attack, Release, Level

Outro

So now you've got everything you need to succeed in the world of Metal, where do you go from here? One thing's for sure - you won't get anywhere (not even to Hell) if you throw on a leather jacket and sing about Satan.

Thankfully, Metal and its related styles are evolving all the time, and although some contemporary bands won't thank you for lumping them in with the hairy Donington-goers of the '70s or the coiffured glamour queens of the '80s, we're still talking about the same thing - loud guitar music with attitude. Many guitarists will tell you that Heavy Metal is dead. It's not - it just got a haircut. Happy bluffing!

If you've enjoyed this book, why not check out the other books in this great new series, available from all good music and book retailers, or in case of difficulty, direct from Music Sales (see page 2).

Blues Guitar	Acoustic Guitar	Rock Guitar	Jazz Guitar	Music Theory
AM955196	AM955174	AM955218	AM955185	AM958485

JOE BENNETT has been teaching guitar for fifteen years, and regularly works as a session guitarist. He is also a senior examiner in electric guitar for The London College of Music and Head of Popular Music at City of Bath College. Joe's publications include the *Guitar: To Go!* and *Really Easy Guitar* series, and *The Little Book of Scales*, plus tracks and articles for *Future Music*, *PowerOn* and *Total Guitar* magazines.